Penguins

Emily Bone

Designed by Will Dawes and Helen Edmonds

Illustrated by Jenny Cooper and Tim Haggerty

Penguin consultants: Dr. Margaret Rostron and Dr. John Rostron
Reading consultant: Alison Kelly, Roehampton University

Contents

What is a penguin?

Penguins are birds with chunky bodies and short, flat wings.

These emperor penguins are the biggest type of penguin.

 Unlike most birds, penguins cannot fly.

Life in the cold

Some penguins live in Antarctica, the coldest place on Earth. Most of the land is covered in thick ice and snow all of the time.

These penguins are standing on a huge floating block of ice called an iceberg.

Penguins' bodies
keep them warm.

A thick layer of fat
under their skin
keeps out the cold.

Tightly-packed
feathers protect
their skin from the
icy wind and water.

They often keep their
wings close to their
bodies to trap heat.

They can tuck their feet
under their warm bodies.

5

Super swimmers

Penguins spend most of their lives at sea. They use their strong wings to swim quickly under the water.

Penguins jump into the sea. They swim underwater and hunt for food.

They dive in and out of the water while they are swimming to rest their wings.

When they have finished hunting, they leap out of the sea onto the ice.

This is a Humboldt penguin.
It has short, smooth feathers
that help it to move through
the water easily.

Sea food

Penguins find all their food at sea. They catch fish, small squid and tiny sea creatures called krill.

This is a Galapagos penguin. As it swims, it catches fish and swallows them whole.

Penguins have hooked beaks to help them grab slippery sea creatures.

They also have spines inside their mouths, so their food can't slip away.

Emperor penguins can go for up to 120 days without food.

Getting warmer

Some penguins live in very warm places, such as New Zealand and South America. They find lots of ways to stay cool.

They hunt at night, when it is cooler.

African penguins live on beaches in South Africa.

Humboldt penguins have bald patches on their faces to help them to stay cool.

Snares Island penguins nest in forests where trees shade them from the hot sun.

On solid ground

When penguins are on land, they have different ways of getting from place to place.

These royal penguins are waddling along a beach. They are holding out their wings to help them balance.

To move quickly, some penguins push themselves across the ice on their bellies.

Their tough feet and sharp claws help them to climb up rocky slopes.

Sometimes, penguins jump across cracks in the ice or hop from rock to rock.

Laying eggs

Every year, penguins gather in huge groups called rookeries to lay eggs.

Some penguins return to the same rookery year after year.

To keep their eggs off the cold ground, most penguins build nests. Different types of penguins use different things for their nests.

In rocky places, penguins pile up stones to make a nest for their eggs.

Some penguins line their nests with grass and feathers to keep their eggs warm.

Other penguins dig burrows in the ground and lay their eggs in them.

Hatching out

Emperor penguins don't make nests. They have to keep eggs warm using their bodies.

A mother emperor penguin lays an egg and places it on the father penguin's feet.

A flap on his tummy keeps the egg warm while the mother leaves to find food.

If there are icy storms, the father penguins huddle in a group to stay warm.

After 60 days, the chick pecks through the egg and climbs out. Then, the mother penguin returns to look after it.

This penguin is balancing a chick on its feet, away from the cold ground.

Growing up

When they are very young, penguin chicks can't feed themselves or swim.

This penguin has swallowed food and is bringing it up as a thick paste to feed to its chicks.

When a penguin
chick is born, it
is covered with
fluffy feathers.

When it is partly
grown, the baby
feathers start to fall
off in patches.

As it grows up,
the penguin gets a
full coat of shiny,
new feathers.

Penguin parents and chicks look so
different, early explorers thought they
were different types of penguins.

Keeping clean

Penguins cover their feathers in oil. This is called preening. It keeps their bodies dry and warm.

A penguin uses its beak to pick up the oil from the skin near its tail.

It runs its beak along every feather so that it is coated in the oil.

Penguins spend a long time preening every day.

These rockhopper penguins are preening each other to clean the feathers they can't reach on their own.

Penguin talk

Penguins use their bodies to tell each other different things.

Gentoo penguins, like these, make honking noises to call to each other.

No two penguins have the same call.

Bwark?

Preetz!

When two penguins bow and flap their wings it shows that they are a pair.

If a penguin is pointing its beak it wants another penguin to go away.

When a chick is hungry and wants to be fed, it taps on its parent's beak.

Enemies

Lots of animals hunt penguins for food.
These animals are called predators.

Leopard seals, like this,
hunt penguins.

1. A skua flies over a rookery looking for penguin eggs to steal and eat.

2. The penguins call loudly and peck at the bird to scare it away.

1. Killer whales hunt penguins when they are swimming through the water.

2. The penguins swim away quickly and leap out onto the ice, away from the whale.

Playing

Sometimes, penguins look as if they are playing but there are good reasons why they act as they do.

Some penguins ride on a wave as if they are surfing. This is the quickest way for them to get back to the land.

Penguin chicks pick up sticks and chase each other, as if they are playing a game. They are actually learning how to make a nest.

Lots of penguins gather on the ice and quickly dive into the sea at the same time. This is to confuse any predators in the water.

Studying penguins

Scientists study penguins on land and in the sea to find out more about them.

Some scientists live for several months in research stations near to where penguins live.

 If people get too close to penguins, they may hit them with their wings.

Scientists measure and weigh penguins to check that they are healthy.

They gently attach tags to penguins that store information about where they go.

A camera is strapped onto a penguin's back to find out what it does underwater.

Scientists also check nests to count how many chicks are born each year.

Glossary

Here are some words in this book you might not know. This page tells you what they mean.

 Antarctica - the coldest place on Earth. Most penguins live here.

 rookery - a place where penguins go to find partners and raise chicks.

 chick - a baby penguin that hatches from an egg.

 preening - covering feathers with oil to keep them warm and dry.

 skua - a large seabird that eats penguin eggs and chicks.

 predator - an animal that catches and kills other animals for food.

 nest - a mound or hollow most penguins build to keep eggs warm.

Websites to visit

You can visit exciting websites to find out more about penguins.

To visit these websites, go to the Usborne Quicklinks Website at **www.usborne-quicklinks.com** Read the internet safety guidelines, and then type the keywords "**beginners penguins**".

The websites are regularly reviewed and the links in Usborne Quicklinks are updated. However, Usborne Publishing is not responsible, and does not accept liability, for the content or availability of any website other than its own. We recommend that children are supervised while on the internet.

This emperor penguin is feeding its chick.

Index

Acknowledgements

Photographic manipulation by John Russell

Photo credits
The publishers are grateful to the following for permission to reproduce material:
© **Corbis/Photolibrary** cover, 1; © **Gallo Images/CORBIS** 10-11 (Martin Harvey);
© **GERALD L KOOYMAN/Animals Animals/Photolibrary** 5;
© **IRA MEYER/National Geographic Stock** 24; © **Jan Vermeer/Minden Pictures/FLPA** 22;
© **JTB Photo/Japan Travel Bureau/Photolibrary** 14; © **Kevin Scafer/NHPA** 21;
© **Konrad Wothe/Minden Pictures/FLPA** 12; © **Maria Stenzel/Corbis** 4;
© **Momatiuk - Eastcott/Corbis** 18; © **NHPA/Photoshot** 2-3 (David Tipling);
© **Pete Oxford/naturepl.com** 8-9; © **sodapix sodapix/F1 Online/Photolibrary** 7;
© **Thorsten Milse/Mauritius/Photolibrary** 31; © **Thorsten Milse/PicturePress/Photolibrary** 17;
© **Wayne Lynch/Arctic Photo** 26; © **www.photo.antarctica.ac.uk** 28.

First published in 2009 by Usborne Publishing Ltd., Usborne House, 83-85 Saffron Hill, London EC1N 8RT,
England. www.usborne.com Copyright © 2009 Usborne Publishing Ltd. The name Usborne and the
devices ⚲⚥ are Trade Marks of Usborne Publishing Ltd. All rights reserved. No part of this publication may
be reproduced, stored in a retrieval system, or transmitted in any form or by any means, electronic,
mechanical, photocopying, recording or otherwise without the prior permission of the publisher.
First published in America 2009. U.E.

Sun, moon and stars

Farm animals

Elizabeth I

RUBBISH AND RECYCLING

Dogs

Horses and ponies

Spiders

Planes

Ancient Greeks

Cats

VOLCANOES

DINOSAURS

Your Body

Armour

Sharks

Celts

Vikings

Castles

How flowers grow

Knights

Living in space

Caterpillars and Butterflies

Ballet

Pirates

Egyptians

Eggs and Chicks

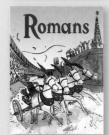
Romans

Weather

Tadpoles and Frogs

Why do we eat?

Under the sea

Bears

Aztecs

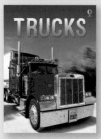
TRUCKS

Night Animals

Firefighters

Antarctica

Bugs

COWBOYS

Planet Earth